GW00706015

DERMOT BOLGER

For Bernadette,
with best
wishes,

Dermot Bolger

THE CHOSEN MOMENT

Met 7th oct '04

NEW ISLAND

THE CHOSEN MOMENT
First published in Ireland in 2004
by New Island,
2 Brookside,
Dundrum Road,
Dublin 14
www.newisland.ie

Signed limited edition published simultaneously in 2004
by Joe McCann, 76 Oliver Road, Oxford, OX4 2JF

ISBN 1 904301 54 1 (New Island)
1 904301 18 5 (Joe McCann)

British Library Cataloguing in Publication Data. A CIP catalogue record for this book is
available from the British Library.

Typeset by New Island
Cover design by New Island
Printed in Ireland by ColourBooks

New Island received financial assistance from
The Arts Council (An Chomhairle Ealaíon), Dublin, Ireland.

10 9 8 7 6 5 4 3 2 1

Contents

In memory
Linda Mullally

Most of these poems were completed in a succession of rooms in All Hallows College in Drumcondra, while the author was a guest writer in that institution. He would like to express his sincere gratitude to everyone within the college for their hospitality and support in creating the conditions of quietude and reflection under which this book and several others have been written.

Acknowledgement is due to the editors of the following where some of these poems first appeared: *The Irish Times, The SHOp magazine, Sunday Independent, Sunday Tribune, A History of Donabate Golf Club, Poetry Salzburg Review.*

THE CHOSEN MOMENT
(For Bernadette)

The second it took for three sailors to sip
The dregs of a war-time round of stout
Made him miss the bus back to his ship:
Made him change vessels, meet a girl, slip
Into the orbit of love that brought me about.

That moment two bicycles slowed to a halt
Outside Trinity College on a January night:
Our future spun like a coin as we thought
To part after several dates, keeping things light,
Unaware we each were what the other sought.

Lives are woven together by intricate layers
Of chance and circumstance: by snap decisions
When love unexpectedly, inexplicably beckons
Through doors opening out into all these years
Hinged on such slim unbeknownst seconds.

THE BAILY LIGHTHOUSE

At times I still dream about the watch room,
Assailed by the spume of waves on every side,
With one and a quarter million candelas
Of power, each fifteen seconds, flashing white,
Forty-one metres above the mean spring tide:
Yielding fourteen and a quarter seconds of darkness
Punctuated by a three-quarter second splurge of light.

During each flash the missing part of me is revealed,
Still hunched there, writing with slow finger strokes
Over the incessant crackle from the short-wave radio.
The part of me that reality could never quite reclaim,
Absorbed in some novel with my back to the window,
Alone with phantoms who keep haunting my brain,
Protected by sea birds and seals on the rocks below.

AFTER THE CHASE

(in memoriam Linda Mullally, 1978–2002)

After the chase through years of watching eyes,
With every warren blocked, every gate closed over,
The world a jerky blur spinning out of focus,
Terrified of bony fingers seizing your shoulder:

For the first time in a decade you pause to breathe
With no fat witch pursuing you, no mocking echo,
Just the sound of your heart allowing itself to rest
And the peace of a pulse that is eternally slow.

The chasing hounds are left behind in the forest
Where low branches snagged your hair and skirt,
Escaping the fairy tale you woke up trapped in
Where down every corridor a trick mirror lurked.

Beyond the forest edge, whether mirage or real,
Lies an ocean, so clear and tantalisingly blue,
That its waters restore a time when you were happy,
They restore to you a time when you were you.

Whales are calling from the depths of clear water,
Amid dolphin-song, in tones you've always known,
You swim above loved ones watching over your bed
To the watchers over them who summon you home.

27 May 2002

Drumcondra Bridge

Three lanes become two here, motorists joist
In a daily game to see who will blink first.

Every afternoon when I approach this bridge
I relive the second when the cyclist strayed
To avoid a pothole that blocked her passage;
Her glimpse of water through the balustrade

As a car brushed the college books on her carrier
With the faintest touch as she swerved and fell.
Traffic crept past while passers-by encircled her
Motionless and hushed as if locked into a spell.

Her back wheel still stun when it had fallen,
With her face hidden, no hint of hair or clothes,
But peeping out from an oil-streaked tarpaulin
Two breathtakingly white slender bare soles.

THE BRIGADIER

(i.m. Francis Stuart)

Dawn. A steep hill into a shadow-strewn glen
Where a military road falls, unearthly straight.
Cradling a white cat, the tall angular man
Descends with his slow, contemplative's gait.

Waiting by the bridge, a brigadier, equally old,
Both veterans of all that there is to be seen.
Neither speaks as the long moments unfold,
Their features gravely inquisitorial yet serene.

"Report, soldier," the brigadier says at length.
"I loved. I made for some small creatures an ark."
"Is that all? Nothing else to cite in your defence?"
Silence. The flicker of a smile. "You may pass."

ABSENT FRIENDS

(For Deirdre)

Dusk on Christmas Eve, a dozen tasks to be done.
The bustle of excited children playing downstairs,
Shopping that needs unpacking, decorations hung.

Amidst that bustle I sometimes find myself alone
In a bedroom, forgetting what I came up to fetch,
As I am swamped by a mosaic of faces once known.

Soon I will go down to celebrate with loved ones,
But I need to recall the shadows who shaped me first.
I open my bedroom window to let absent friends come.

APPROACHING FORTY

(For Robbie Collins & Paddy Farrell)

The younger men fall off on nights like this.
At first nobody appears in the teeming hail
As floodlights illuminate the vacant pitch.
Then slowly a handful of cars start to show.
Drivers stare out at the February gale,
Each exchanging a look through their window.

Surely nobody in their sane mind would play ball
On a night when not even a dog would stir,
But then one door opens and slagging voices call
To ageing men with bad backs and strapped ankles,
Who clamber out to stretch and laugh at the downpour,
Knowing they won't enjoy Fridays like this forever.

6 February 1999

REMEMBERING CERTAIN GOLF HOLES

(For Roger)

Most are forgotten before you reach the next tee.
Encounters, not as brief as they might have been;
A minutiae of drives, chips and scrambled bogeys.

But certain holes resurface in your mind at night:
That stillness at the pitch of a perfect swing,
Rushes and swamp, trees split by shafting light,

Pussy Willow billowing wild in some ditch.
The instant when a white ball soared or rolled
And life elsewhere momentarily ceased to exist.

Often you lie awake, longing to replay some shot
With what fragment of sense you've since picked up.
But you would happily repeat every single mistake

For the moment you carried the lake and yellow furze
Onto a fairway curving past trees placed to punish
Shots that avoided taking on the nest of bunkers.

You watched your ball rise, like a bird taking fright,
And get lost against the blue of an evening skyline,
Where you were lost too, within the arc of its flight.

THE LADY CAPTAIN

Something about how the slant of light
Through a maze of briars and hawthorn
Casts its shifting mesh of shadows
On the mud-churned path to the tee-box
Always flashes back the flecks of sunlight
On the boy's face when she saw him lie
Staring upwards as though amazed
By the blueness of the Kerry sky.

No one was present that morning
Except her and the slain youth
Who had jumped out from a ditch,
Confident that no cars ever drove
Up the unpaved mountain track
Which she turned down by mistake,
So absorbed in studying her map
That she had precious time to brake.

Although it was five decades ago
The longest seconds one could endure
Still lurk here to take her prisoner
When she passes by this hedgerow.
Seconds from a life never mentioned
To her late husband and her son
From whom she hid the numb core
Where her soul had once belonged.

She saw the boy's bemused stare
In the eyes of her first granddaughter,
Glimpsed him on bustling escalators
As his double continued to haunt her
Through five decades without absolution.
Slowly however she made herself forget
And focused on the person she became:
Wife and mother, former lady golf captain.

But during some Tuesday foursomes
When the sun slants like this,
The shadows on the mud track
Force her to catch her breath
And remember how she once knelt
To cradle him like a first born
Beneath the blue of a Kerry sky
Framed by flowers of hawthorn,

And how this child's ghost knows her
In ways her family have never done,
So that he seems like an old flame
Waiting for her to enter his kingdom.
Her golfing partners chatter beside her
Reaching the next tee on the back nine.
Bracing herself against an old pain,
She carves a five iron into the wind.

POET OF THE 1950S

Out of print and out of mind since your death,
Yet your rapt lyrics still reside like fugitives
Inside shrewd anthologies of modern Irish verse.

Vessels for your love, fragility and indignation,
Crafted in decreasing circles where you flitted
From boardroom to hunt ball to discreet asylum.

In the local golf club some older men still recall
Your sports car and dancing with your daughter.
They never knew you wrote or heard of any fame:

They only heard the retort of the single gunshot
And found your body lying against the door-frame.

THE WEDDING PHOTOGRAPH

The cake is multi-tiered, the car sleek and long,
But nothing can outdo the extraordinary smile
Of the luminous bride in her wedding gown

As she stares beyond the camera into a future
With a handsome groom soon who would die of cancer,
Leaving her widowed with eleven young children,

The youngest in his cot when his father dies.
Quietly she got on with raising a proud family,
Twice daily navigating the supermarket aisles.

She died in a Dublin hospital, bereft of repose,
Disbelieving nurses snapping at her to be quiet
When her internal ailments went undiagnosed.

Yet in this picture of them at the wedding car
It is her smile that I immediately recognise.
It never changed throughout decades of toil,

Greeting me each morning on my way to school,
No less radiant that when she posed as a bride
Eager to embrace whatever fate love entailed.

WORDS IN 19TH CENTURY COPIES OF THE ANNALS FOR PROPAGATION OF THE FAITH, THE ATTIC, ALL HALLOWS SEMINARY

(For Anthony Draper)

Perhaps all words eventually share our fate.
Stacked among bric-a-brac, obsolete maps
And photos of dead men with no descendants.

Workmen have punched holes in the brickwork
To overhaul Victorian plumbing and dry rot,
Exposing innards of cables and smashed ballcocks.

Amid this rubble we reside, beside stacked crates
Of *Duffy's Weekly Volume of Catholic Divinity*,
Here in *The Annals for Propagation of the Faith.*

Long-robed correspondents laboured at our birth,
Fishermen of a lost empire, servants of certitude,
Casting their luminous nets over desert and bush.

Entreating readers to pray, they record their catch,
How a woman hid holy water beneath her cloak
To snatch the pagan soul of a dying child for Christ.

We were salmon, somehow finding a route home
From the open sewers of diseased shantytowns
To the seminary corridors where we were spawned

Amid silent prayer in bare cells lit by a tallow dip,
During solitary games of handball in the sleety rain
And rapt nights spent kneeling on stone in worship.

Corralled by their full stops, anchored to this page,
We cannot betray if, with their final rasping breath,
Our authors saw Christ stride or sink through the waves.

The logbooks of floundered ships, yellow with age,
We are beached on shelves beneath arched rafters,
In the belly of this whale with a wooden ribcage.

KEEPERS OF THE BAILY LIGHT
(For Bill Long)

The keepers are gone, this watchroom deserted.
Just a few books left in the small wall cabinet
Marked *Carnegie Libraries for Lighthouse Service*:

A crime paperback, Lloyd's Register of Ships,
Her Majesty's Sea Captain's Medical Guide
And a 1955 Radio Signals Admiralty List.

Four times a minute a three-quarter second flash
Ranges across sandbanks, drifting nets and unlit buoys
To where twice each sixteen seconds the Kisk replies.

A fly settles on a daybook crammed with letters,
Berating P Cunningham in 1959 for taking a taxi
From Crookhaven to Cork when a bus was cheaper,

Cutting L.J. Kennedy's 1966 hackney fare in half,
Requesting personnel to wear white-topped caps
And S. O'Sullivan to vaccinate against small pox.

These folded letters, the brisk officious terms
Are the sole remnants of the confraternity of men
Who struggled with solitude, gales and regulations.

But microscopic clues remain in their fingerprints
That annotate the margins of curt communiqués
Like the notes bored scribes left on medieval gospels.

Thoughts pinned like moths in each crinkled fold:
"I crave wood to carve with, I crave my children."
"I only feel safe here beyond the world's reach."

"Christ, I can't bear another watch on my own,
  Lights of distant ships in this prison of silence,
    I want to scream and tear these walls down."

"The doctors and their tests, maybe they are wrong."
  "My son is drinking hard and I can't stop him,
    I could not be there and now the chance is gone."

The trapped fly takes flight, its buzzing magnified,
In that curved room where men played solitaire,
By the vast unlit windows bereft of watching eyes.

MIDNIGHT NOTES FOR A PAINTER

(For Donnacha and Diarmuid)

The lane behind my house is lit
  By the glow that snow provides,
There is no moon yet in the park
  I clearly spy the playground slides.

No crisp footfalls have disfigured
  The underlay where my dog and I
Walk in a muted sheen of brightness
  Shining from the ground and not the sky.

A Steep Lane in Monaghan

(i.m. Patrick Flanagan)

Who can measure the journey undergone
From being carried up this steep lane by your father

After baptism to his remote hillside farm,
To being carried from that farmhouse by your sons

Out into the dark of a gale-force storm
To be borne down the same lane on their shoulders

Past neighbours with true appreciation
Of eight decades spent traversing eight hundred yards.

November 2002

LET THERE BE SPACE

(For Kazem Sharahari)

Let there be space for an apricot tree to grow:
Once such space exists it can become home.
Each night in your Parisian courtyard you go

To touch the soft fruit and survey the firmament
That framed these same constellations over Persia
In a childhood with no thoughts of imprisonment,

Police beatings and a torturous walk into exile.
Your children dream in French, walk to school
Through babbling immigrant tongues along miles

Of steep cobbled streets and old apartments.
But behind your small gate this garden exists,
A miracle of space where one can write and think

In Persian and French and no known tongue,
Just an empty lexicon straining to be filled
By your children's voices that call it home.

At Twenty

She said, "*I'm suffering from the most terrible flu,*
If we sleep together I'll pass it on to you."

He lay in bed for four days after she left,
Shivering and waking up drenched in sweat,
His throat raw, legs unable to take his weight:
He paid this price happily, with no regret.

THE HUNTED FOX

Some other family will occupy this house then,
Another boy imagine the garden to be his,
Fresh sets of shadows will dart between pillars
After a football barely visible in the darkness.

Generations after them will also glance up from games,
Not registering this return to the street of their birth
Of strangers who gaze up at the windows of bedrooms
That they once regarded as their sanctuary on earth.

THE SECRET ISLAND

While you were sleeping the chance came and passed
During the seconds when you finally relaxed your guard.

For years in your crow's nest you spied on distant shores,
Confident of recognising the destination marked as yours

Your vigil grew into a drug, from dawn to the evening star,
Becoming a connoisseur of delay, a procrastination master.

Now you wake to find that you have sailed beyond
The coves of that secret island glimpsed on the rise,

Where streams gush and trees are bent by the wind
That sprays cold spume against your disbelieving eyes.

Hungary, July 2003

STRANGERS

(i.m. Bridie Bolger & Mary Clifton)

In Baggot Street during the war they surely pass,
Two girls from Monaghan and Cavan farms
Working in Dublin as a waitress and a nurse.

They register their similarities with one glance,
Before hurrying on, wrapped up in separate lives.
They never knew one another or had a chance

To hold the grandsons whom they share.
Both died too young, consumed with worry
For children left behind and by cancer.

I light two white candles side by side for them
At the shrine of St Theresa de L'enfant Jesus
In the hushed cathedral of Our Lady of Reims.

Verses Put Aside Between My 40th and 41st Birthdays

So much time wasted in so many rooms.
    I am half my father's age now.
His sea voyages are over, the swell
    Of tides rolling beneath his bow;
The creak of ships tossed about
    On storm lashed straits.
He has time for whiskey in an easy chair
    Visiting the homes of his children
To savour life as a wise King Lear.

My sons play at being chefs while I type,
    Cooking imaginary pizzas in the wardrobe:
Their calls echo through this old terraced house.

There have been so many rooms, such time wasted.
    So many locations I could enumerate:
Lists of dates, completed books, reassuring facts
    To fill the vanished space of four decades.
Is that me, aged nineteen, lying stretched
    On a table in a courthouse canteen,
Slipping down early to brew tea for break?
    I listen to criminals in the corridor chat
Before the duty guard announces their case.
    Time is a prison that ticks slowly there,
Needing to be snatched during office hours
    Which I spend burning boxes on the skite,
Or skiving among books on the court balcony
    Watching the judge impersonate Mr Punch.

But I'm too far ahead, I need to skip back,
    Past the stacked pallets in the factory
Where I hang loose with Eugene chewing hash

While the long night shift drags past
Like an ancient tortoise, torturously slow,
As we wait for skylights to lighten.
I am awaiting the bell in a Finglas classroom,
Waiting to turn twelve years of age,
Falling back to the infinity of a day playing
With pegs as my mother hangs washing.
That's me down there, or at least I think so,
In the boxroom with the ventilation hole
Through which I'm terrified ghosts will enter.
I close my eyes, pull the blankets tighter,
Afraid to turn and see what horrors lurk there.
What am I scared of, what can I remember
Amid nightmares of snakes slithering on the lino?
Crying in the dark that I have no friends,
Crying in the dark that I am not good enough.
Curling up in the blankets like an embryo.

I roll four socks into a ball and throw it,
It hits the wall and spins back
For me to volley into the net for Ireland.
Children play outside on the road.
My mother is dead. Alone in the house,
I toss the ball against the wall and score.

I pace empty rooms, the twelve-year-old curator
Of the house where I was born
After a midwife untangled the cord choking me.
Every room contains a separate fear,
The pig's face glimpsed at an upstairs window,
The waiting figure on the bottom stair.

I lock the bathroom door, imagining whispers
From the attic or closed wardrobe
Where I hung my father's black mourning tie.
Nights alone, conjuring fantasies,

With the huge typewriter my brother procured
    Filling the silence with clamorous keys.

Rooms untidy as my plans, father at sea, siblings married.
    When I cannot afford a typewriter ribbon,
I type the ghosts of poems on carbon paper copies.
    Finding work, I block out light to sleep,
Then wake and write before the night shift starts,
    Returning at dawn through white frost.

Fast-forward eleven years, our first child being born,
    More frozen roads as I wave a taxi down,
We take him home and kneel, to peer into his carrycot,
    As if he were a bomb about to burst.
I tried to imagine my son and I being forty and ten:
    They seem impossible ages back then,
Wheeling him in the park, letting him down to crawl,
    Longing for him to learn to walk
Like the toddler under the trees kicking football.

Yet, miraculously, we're here now, aged forty and ten.
    Time has pushed on with bewildering pace
To this threshold of the twenty-first millennium,
    In which the world invests such significance.
But no spin-doctor can dictate the landmarks of a life,
    The few moments recalled in sharp relief
Amidst the minutiae that soon fades into oblivion.

At the end of my century, which my sons partly shared,
    I see theirs start to glimmer like a tiny pearl.
What can I tell them about mine? What can I pass on,
    Swamped in this age of incessant facts,
With truth buried under a million instant photographs?
    All I have learnt is how little I know.
At the end of a century that stopped making sense
    I wish only to hold their growing hands
And marvel at the magnitude of my own ignorance.

And at the miracle – which I could not have imagined
As a youth walking the streets of Finglas
Every night, pacing out in my mind the metre of verse
As a poultice against my loneliness –
That I would find love and somebody to share my life,
To watch over me, understand how I move
Between two worlds at once, needing my daily ration
Of three meals, a thousand words and love.

Closing my eyes now, I listen to my sons at play
And recall the dream last night where I stood
In my father's overgrown garden beside the girl
Who helped me plant a chestnut sprig
Given to us once by an old Protestant neighbour.
In my dream the sprig blocked out the sky
As we stood beneath it, three decades later,
To stare in awe at the maze of branches
That seemed to make sense of our lives since then.

Yet, although we were aware of adult histories,
The girl in my dream had not changed.
Gazing at her nine-year-old china features,
I felt simultaneously a child and a man.
In adolescence we lost touch with one another,
Venturing forth into the adult world,
But this dream threw us back together
With the marvellous ease of childhood.

We felt no need to exchange one single word.
We stared at the tree we had planted
And amid that lush greenness before I woke,
I felt such intense consolation
At this chestnut soaring into the Finglas sky,
With the span of each branch
Celebrating another year in the long march
Gradually sapping our strength.
Because, defying time, the moment still existed

When in the sunlight we began to run,
Carrying a sprig from an old man's garden
Across the heart-stopping world of the young.